What Kind of Animal Is It?

Animals Called Fish

Kristina Lundblad & Bobbie Kalman

A Crabtree Crown Book

Crabtree Publishing
crabtreebooks.com

Animals Called Fish

Editor-in-chief
Bobbie Kalman

Writing team
Kristina Lundblad
Bobbie Kalman

Substantive editor
Kelley MacAulay

Editors
Molly Aloian
Reagan Miller
Kathy Smithyman

Design
Samara Parent

Consultant
Luke K. Butler, Ph.C., Department of Biology and Burke Museum of Natural History, University of Washington

Production manager
Candice Campbell

Photographs
Wikimedia Commons : ©Roger Sweeting : page 28 (bottom); ©Peter Southwood : page 29 (bottom); Shutterstock

Illustrations
Katherine Kantor : pages 5, 29 (top);
Cori Marvin : page 11 (bottom)

Crabtree Publishing

crabtreebooks.com 800-387-7650

In Canada: We acknowledge the financial support of the Government of Canada through the Canada Book Fund for our publishing activities.

Printed in the U.S.A./CP032026

Published in Canada
Crabtree Publishing
616 Welland Ave.
St. Catharines,
Ontario L2M 5V6

Published in the United States
Crabtree Publishing
347 Fifth Ave.
Suite 1402-145
New York, NY 10016

Hardcover: 978-1-0398-7313-1
Paperback: 978-1-0398-7371-1
Ebook (pdf): 978-1-0398-7420-6
Epub: 978-1-0398-7469-5

Library and Archives Canada Cataloguing in Publication
Available at Library and Archives Canada

Library of Congress Cataloging-in-Publication Data
Available at the Library of Congress

Contents

Fantastic fish!

Fish are animals that live in water. Fish live in water all over the world. Some fish are small, and other fish are big. There are three main groups of fish.

damselfish

goldfish

lionfish

Bony fish

One group of fish is called **bony fish**. Most fish belong to this group. The damselfish, goldfish, and lionfish on this page are bony fish. Read more about bony fish on pages 24 and 25.

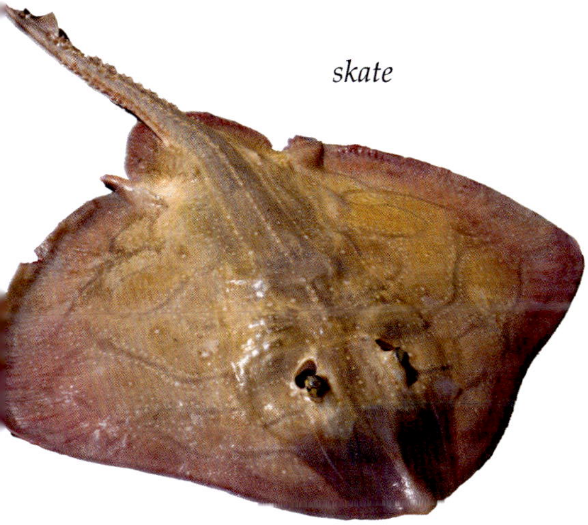
skate

shark

Skeletons made of cartilage

Sharks, skates, and rays belong to another group of fish. These fish have skeletons that are made of **cartilage**. Cartilage can bend. Read more about these fish on pages 26 and 27.

ray

hagfish

lamprey

Jawless fish

Hagfish and lampreys make up a group of fish called **jawless fish**. Read more about jawless fish on pages 28 and 29.

A fish's body

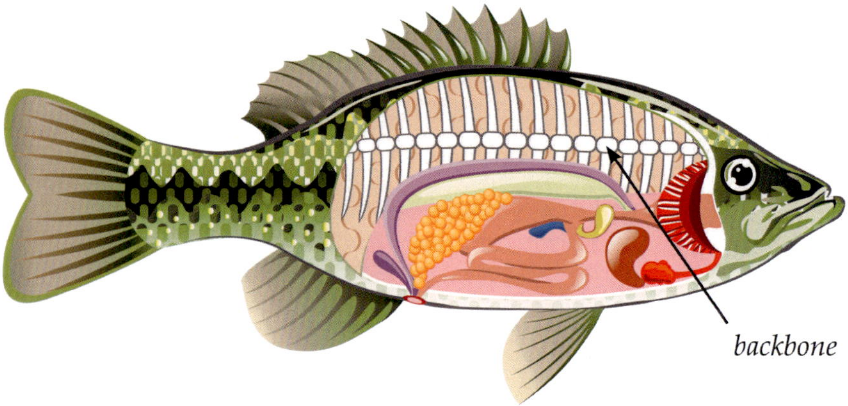

Fish have **backbones** inside their bodies. A backbone is made up of bones that run down the middle of an animal's back.

Fish have scales

Most fish have **scales** all over their bodies. Scales cover and protect their skin. The colors, shapes, and sizes of scales can be different. Some fish have small, smooth scales. Other fish have large, rough scales.

Look at a close-up picture of a fish's scales!

Some fish change colors as they grow older. This young angelfish will change color as it grows older.

Cold blood

Fish are **cold-blooded** animals. The body of a cold-blooded animal stays about the same temperature as the place where the animal lives. If a fish lives in cold water, its body is cold. If a fish lives in warm water, its body is warm.

This fish is a lingcod. It lives in cold water, so its body is cold.

Clown fish live in warm water. Their bodies are warm.

Fish have gills

All animals must breathe **oxygen** to survive. Oxygen is a gas that is a part of air. It is also a part of water. Fish use body parts called **gills** to breathe the oxygen in water.

Gills are openings on the sides of a fish's body. You can see the gills through this fish's mouth.

What are gills?

To breathe in oxygen, a fish opens its mouth and sucks in water. The water flows over its gills. The gills pull oxygen from the water. To breathe out, a fish closes its mouth and pushes water out through its gills.

*Most fish have **gill covers**. Gill covers are flaps of skin on top of the gills. Gill covers protect the gills.*

Using its gills

When a fish breathes in, water goes into its mouth. The fish's gills are closed.

When a fish breathes out, its gills open and its mouth closes.

How do fish swim?

The bodies of fish are built for swimming. They are smooth and narrow. Fish bodies are also covered with **mucus**. Mucus is a slimy coating that helps fish glide through water.

A fish has strong muscles on the sides of its body. These muscles help the fish swim.

Fish fins

Fish have fins on their bellies, backs, and sides. Their tails are also fins! Some fins are big. Other fins are small. Fish swim by moving their fins. They use them to turn, to stop, and to move forward.

Salt water

Different kinds of fish live in different **habitats**. A habitat is the natural place where an animal lives. Most fish live in oceans. The water in oceans is salty. Some parts of oceans are deep and cold. Other parts of oceans are shallow and warm.

Anglerfish live deep in oceans. The deep parts of oceans are cold, dark, and quiet. Very few plants grow in the deep parts of oceans.

Some fish live in both shallow water and deep water. This barracuda sometimes lives in deep water. At other times, it lives in shallow water.

Coral reefs

Many fish and plants live in coral reefs. Coral reefs are in warm, shallow waters. They are colorful places. The coral reef shown on this page is full of different kinds of fish!

Fresh water

Some fish live in rivers, lakes, ponds, and swamps. These habitats have fresh water. Fresh water does not have salt. Most habitats with fresh water are not as deep as habitats that have salt water.

Carp live in lakes, rivers, and ponds. Carp often flop around in mud to dig up small animals to eat.

Many trout live in streams. The water in streams moves quickly. These trout have long, strong bodies for swimming.

A few types of fish can live in both fresh water and salt water. Salmon are born in streams that have fresh water. They swim a long way to live in oceans.

Fish food

Fish must eat to stay alive. Different fish eat different foods. Many fish that live in fresh water eat plants. Many plants grow in fresh water, so the fish have plenty to eat.

This fish is a tilapia. It lives in fresh water. It eats plants and other animals.

Meat-eating fish

Most fish that live in oceans hunt and eat other animals. Animals that hunt and eat other animals are called **predators**. The animals predators eat are called **prey**. Most fish that are predators have sharp teeth and strong jaws for catching prey.

Spotted goatfish are predators. They eat other animals.

Moray eels are predators. They use their long, sharp teeth to eat octopuses and fish.

Staying safe

Fish have different ways of staying safe from predators. Some fish swim so quickly that very few predators can catch them.

Other fish hide from predators. These fish hide by blending in with the rocks, coral, or plants around them.

This fish is a brown coney. Its body blends in with the colors of the rocks in its habitat. Blending in helps the fish hide from predators.

A group of fish that swims together is called a **school**. *Swimming in a school helps fish stay safe. A school of fish looks like one big fish. Most predators do not attack such big fish.*

Sharp spines

Some fish stay safe by having **spines** on their bodies. Spines are body parts shaped like sharp needles. This porcupine fish swallows water to make its body bigger. Once it is puffed up, predators can see the sharp spines on its body! Sharp spines make the fish hard to eat, so most predators stay away from it.

Fish eggs

Most fish lay eggs. Some fish lay a few eggs at a time. Other fish lay thousands of eggs at once! Some baby fish hatch from their eggs after only one or two days. Other baby fish take a few months to hatch.

(left) Not all baby fish hatch at the same time! This baby salmon just broke out of its egg. The other babies have not yet hatched.

These baby rainbow trout are hatching from their eggs!

Protecting the eggs

Many kinds of animals eat fish eggs. Some fish protect their eggs so the eggs will not be eaten! Many fish hide their eggs in mud. Some fish hide their eggs in their mouths. Other fish carry their eggs in pouches on their bodies.

This male jawfish is carrying his eggs in his mouth!

Most fish do not look after their babies. After hatching, baby fish must take care of themselves. This young sheephead fish is looking for food.

Bony fish

There are more bony fish than there are any other kinds of fish. The skeleton of a bony fish is made of hard bones. The outside of its body is covered with smooth, thin scales. Parrotfish are bony fish.

parrotfish

A lionfish is a dangerous bony fish! It has sharp spines on its body. There is poison in the spines.

This fancy goldfish is a bony fish. Many people keep goldfish as pets in fish tanks.

A butterfly fish is a bony fish. Its body is round and thin. Its mouth is pointed. A butterfly fish pushes its mouth between rocks and plants to find food.

Bones that bend

Sharks, rays, and skates belong to another group of fish. The skeletons of these fish are made of cartilage. Cartilage is light, and it bends. Your ears are made of cartilage. Having light skeletons that bend allows sharks, rays, and skates to move easily in water.

The skin of sharks, rays, and skates looks smooth, but it is covered with rough scales.

Shark babies

Some baby sharks do not hatch from eggs. They are **born live.** Animals that are born live are not inside eggs when they come out of their mothers' bodies.

Skates and rays

Skates and rays have wide, flat bodies. They have big fins that look like wings. Their flat bodies glide easily along the bottom of the ocean. The colors of skates and rays are the same as the colors of the sand and rocks on the ocean floor. Blending in helps these fish hide so they can catch their prey.

A stingray has a poisonous spine on its tail. It uses the spine to sting predators.

This skate's body is the same color as the sand on the ocean floor.

Jawless fish

Hagfish and lampreys are jawless fish. They make up the smallest group of fish. Jawless fish do not have jaws. Jaws are bones that hold an animal's teeth. Instead of jaws, a jawless fish has a round mouth. It uses its mouth to suck in food.

The Pacific lamprey has tiny teeth inside its mouth. The teeth cut into the skin of its prey. The lamprey then sucks the prey's blood.

This sea lamprey has sunk its teeth into a bony fish. It is sucking the blood of the fish.

Smooth skin

The skeletons of jawless fish are made of cartilage, just like the skeletons of sharks, skates, and rays. Jawless fish are not covered with scales. They have smooth, slimy skin.

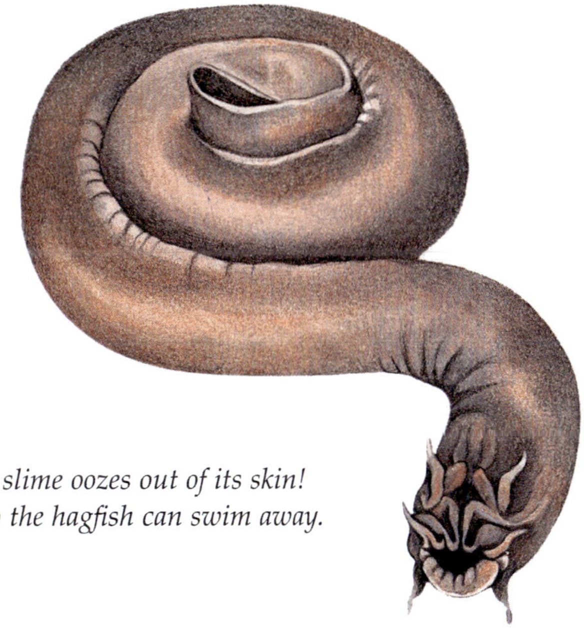

When a hagfish is in danger, slime oozes out of its skin! The slime traps the predator, so the hagfish can swim away.

Hagfish are nearly blind! They find food by using their senses of touch and smell.

Is it a fish?

Fish live in waters all over the world, but not every animal that lives in water is a fish! The animals on these pages live in water. Guess which animals are fish and which are not fish!

A sea horse may not look like other fish, but it is a bony fish!

Are crabs fish?

Crabs are not fish. Fish have backbones. Crabs do not have backbones. Crabs belong to a group of animals called **crustaceans**. Crustaceans have hard coverings on their bodies. They do not have scales, as fish do.

Are sea stars fish?

Some people call these animals starfish, but sea stars are not fish. Sea stars do not have backbones. The bodies of sea stars are covered in sharp spikes. The spikes make it hard for predators to eat sea stars.

humpback whale

Are whales fish?

Whales live in oceans, but they are not fish. Whales are **mammals**. Mammals do not use gills to breathe, as fish do. Whales breathe using **lungs**, just as you do. Lungs are body parts that take in air and let out air.

Words to know and Index